GOAL SETTING STRENGTH

Best Practices to Reach Your Goals by Staying in the Action and Out of the Result!

Blaire Camarda, CPT, CSCS

Copyright © 2021 Coach Blaire Camarda, CPT, CSCS

All rights reserved. No part of this book may be reproduced or used in any manner without written permission of the copyright owner except for the use of quotations in a book review. For more information, address: clearstrength@outlook.com.

First paperback edition January 2021

Imprint: Independently published

Book design and cover design by Ana Kreker

ISBN: 9798597964560

"The information in this book is a gold mine! Coach Blaire really provides actionable ways to help the reader not only move forward in the direction of their own progress but also be their own accountability coach for the areas they are personally looking to improve in life. Beware, though, this read is only for those who are ready to accept the change that will provide them better processes and outcomes in the life they are working towards."

-Ricky Martinez

Founder of The Players Promise and Athlete Development Specialist

"This book is unique in the sense that it shows you how to apply the information that you may have already come across, along your journey, to better yourself. You may have the knowledge to move forward and work on yourself, but this will give you the tools to actually apply that knowledge to your own life and hold yourself accountable. It will give you confidence and keep you on track!"

-C.A.C

Yoga Instructor

"Blaire's ability to dig deep and offer clear, straight-forward processes to effectively tackle challenges and obstacles provides a light at the end of the tunnel for anyone feeling stuck and overwhelmed. I use the strategies in this book with my clients and higher-level athletes to help gain focus and perspective throughout their training programs."

-Rory Glover

Personal Trainer and Track Coach

"This book hits you like a much-needed slap in the face from your best friend: funny, honest, and thought-provoking. Only read this book if you are willing to ditch your excuses and take an active role in your own success."

-Elizabeth Burd

Entrepreneur and marathoner

Also by BLAIRE CAMARDA

MOTIVATIONAL STRENGTH

For everyone who ever wanted to be and to do better, but was unsure how to get there.

THE INSIDES

PART 1

WHAT IS CLEAR STRENGTH	9
LOVE, COACH BLAIRE	11
PREFACE	15
SET THE STAGE	19

PART 2

1	CATEGORY 1: ACTIVITY AND EXERCISE	25
2	BENEFITS	31
3	REWARDS	37
4	CATEGORY 2: HEALTH AND EATING HABITS	43
5	ADDITIONAL GOALS	47
6	CHALLENGES AND SOLUTIONS	51
7	EVALUATION OF GOALS	63
8	RECAP	67

PART 3

GOAL WORKSHEET	69
ACKNOWLEDGEMENTS	73

WHAT IS CLEAR STRENGTH

"Stay in the action and out of the result."

- Coach Blaire Camarda

WHAT IS CLEAR STRENGTH?

CLEAR STRENGTH (CS) is a community of like-minded individuals looking to increase their strength in all ways: emotional, mental, spiritual, and physical. This is a place for those who want to learn more about strength training, strength sports, and how to be their own version of an ultimate bad ass! No gimmicks, no fluff. Uncomplicated, straight forward, and CLEAR strategies so you enhance your habits, take your goal achievements, and your life, to the next level! We are constantly surrounded by recommendations about how to approach health and fitness or weight loss or business on all platforms of social media, TV, podcasts, radio, etc., but we are missing one major component. We don't always get the information on **how-to** apply said recommendations. Clear Strength is your **how-to**!

By pulling back the curtain, removing the sugar coating, and laying out a clear path to get it done, you will see that making progress is manageable and you CAN do great things! Your efforts and potential will be amplified by the skills you will strengthen in this community. Understand that you have a great opportunity and the ability to change your life. If you are open to change and looking to contribute to creating mutual bad-assery, you are in the right place!

At CS, we believe the way you do one thing is the way you do most things. That means you must set yourself up for ultimate success from the beginning! No cutting corners. In this community we provide you concrete plans to strengthen your skillsets, enhance your behaviors, and get the most out of yourself. The skills you develop in the CS community can be applied to any other goals you want to reach, in any area of your life. In this particular series, we discuss topics such as, how to create motivation from within, how confidence increases with follow-through, how emotional tenacity surfaces in workouts, and much more. You will strengthen your approach to goal setting, understand how to generate your path of effective actions, and continue your personal growth. We want you to have all the information possible so you can create and live your best life!

How to contact Clear Strength:

Email: clearstrength@outlook.com

LOVE, COACH BLAIRE

"You are stronger than you believe. You have greater powers than you know."

-Wonder Woman

LOVE, COACH BLAIRE

Dear Fellow Goal Crusher,

Let's start with a little about me so you aren't talking to a stranger. My name is Blaire Camarda, and I am a female fitness pro living with and working with Fibromyalgia and chronic pelvic issues. Chronic pain has changed every aspect of my life.

However, when I decided to become my own best advocate, let go of what I cannot control, and to get the most out of my life I knew I had to let in change. By focusing on what I can do and what I want to accomplish, I began to allow change into my life. This meant I became willing to shift my approach to life and began to give myself permission to get comfortable being uncomfortable. I began to learn how to work in harmony with my circumstances to provide *myself* the opportunity to continue moving forward. In turn, the strategies in the chapters ahead have affected my emotional, mental, and spiritual strength in a great way. As a by-product of manifesting emotional, mental, and spiritual strength I produced a great deal of increased physical strength. Before I could expect anything different, I had to be willing to change my mindset and my actions.

I have overcome injuries and surgeries courtesy of contact sports and not-so-great training during my youth, but chronic disease and inflammation are different. Over the years, I've had to develop a new understanding of how to set goals that made sense and didn't only sound nice. For a long time, I didn't even realize I wasn't doing it right. I, like many people, would know what I wanted and then repeat a cycle of frustration, habit breakdown, and "restarting" when things did not work out. Never again. No more restarting. Only course correction until, well...forever.

One major point I want you to remember throughout this book is that: **You must know your goal to understand your path.** Otherwise, you are wandering around without direction executing "drive-by goal setting" and have no real idea of how to get where you say you want to go. Therefore, I want to share with you what helped me to not only talk the talk but learn to walk the walk. To hone my goal-setting skills, I lay out clear and concise action steps (smaller goals) and an individualized rewards system paired with a timeline to review and evaluate how well my blueprint is working. I also identify obstacles I can foresee and how I will overcome them. This allows me to minimize roadblocks and plateaus in my training and personal development.

When I started to implement this process on a regular basis, I began staying on track more consistently and for longer periods of time. I felt more empowered to overcome unforeseen obstacles and felt more in control (even during times of major change). I also became prouder of my mindset and internal resilience. My focus became consistency, not perfection—another recurring theme you will find in this book. This system has helped me, and my clients, get results that last. I want you to be able to benefit from it as well. Before starting out, understand your expections of: (1) what you expect of yourself/the standard you will hold yourself to and (2) how you will process your actual experience if it is different than what you expect. You will build credibility and confidence within yourself by following through, and having a better understanding of your expectations will help you do just that!

The experiences you create mean something! Take pride in the fact that you can create opportunities to enrich your life. The circumstances surrounding each of us are different, but when you understand how to set effective goals that are customized, for just you, and have a secure, adjustable, system in place to make it happen, you have a more meaningful experience and continue to get results! You build credibility with yourself because when you follow through, you prove to yourself that you can handle change and thrive during times of transformation. Speaking of change, we are in the middle of a freaking pandemic so, what better time to "get good" at change?

This is your opportunity to take a step closer to greater internal resilience, strengthening your self-awareness, and proving that you can take back your personal power to live your life with confidence and conviction! Don't wait for the perfect time to start making plans and setting goals. That perfect time doesn't exist. It is up to you to create your ideal time with the energy and focus you bring. It is up to you to walk with the willingness to work through adversity and improve along the way. You never need perfection, only consistency. Take the pressure of perfection off yourself and understand that you have the power to influence your environment and the life you want.

I hope this book provides you the platform to take your goal setting to the next level by enhancing your skillset and your opportunities to embrace lasting results by staying in the action! Let's do this!

Love, Coach Blaire

PREFACE

"The most effective way to do it, is to do it."

-Amelia Earhart

PREFACE

Don't expect anyone to want your goals more than you. The goal-setting strategies laid out in this book can be used in other areas of your life—not only your health and fitness. After reviewing the process of these goal-setting strategies, go back and see where you can apply the same processes to other areas of your life. You may have business or personal development goals on the radar that are worth pursuing. To make this system fit, simply modify the category spotlights listed at the beginning of the next chapter and BAM, you've got a tailored goal-setting strategy for any area of your life.

For the sake of this conversation, we will keep the focus around health and fitness. I highly encourage you to think outside the box as you go through this process so that your internal investments can be applied effectively. In other words, don't half-ass it. Please use your full ass. Thinking outside the box does not need to create complications. Even one behavioral enhancement can create a massive positive ripple effect. Simplicity is key.

We must shed some light on what will make or break this process, and that is change. Effects of change manifest differently for everyone in the mental, physical, emotional, and spiritual bodies. Change often creates obstacles which lead to larger roadblocks within a health and fitness program. If you aren't willing to embrace change, you experience more setbacks and longer delays in reaching your goals. Sometimes, you must go a little below the surface to see more than simply squeezing in a workout. Change in life is inevitable and how you respond to it creates your future. You are responsible for creating your path. You must be able to "see" it, to understand it. How you respond to your obstacles determines your outcome far more than what the obstacle itself determines. This is where goal setting and a kick-ass coach help you navigate this adventure.

You must know your goal to understand your path. Once you understand your path, decide to use *structured flexibility* so you strengthen your ability to roll with the punches. Life happens and *structured flexibility* provides you the safety net to have structure and to persist when things don't quite go according to plan. *Structured flexibility* also allows you the space for creativity along the way. It is helpful to focus on constructive efforts instead of perfection; and you can minimize your setbacks by executing a willingness to make mistakes, evaluate your progress, and course correct along the way.

By trial, error, and over many years, I have established this system of guiding myself and my clients to set realistic <u>goals</u> that are specific, measurable, and achievable. We work together to identify the <u>benefits</u> that will be experienced when, *not if,* the goals are achieved. We then lay out how <u>rewards</u> will be implemented, in a **"non-edible"** way, as a tool of acknowledgement of positive efforts and actions. "Non-edible" might sound weird now, but it won't in a few chapters. After we understand the rewards system, we work to identify the <u>challenges</u> that could create difficulty for the goals to be reached and then we commit to <u>overcoming</u> the identified challenges, with a 1:1 ratio. These elements are non-negotiable. Keep in mind that there is some pliability with the categories—based on your individual needs, goals and the subject, or direction, of your specific aspirations.

Although tricky at times, you still harness the ability to take hold of your own personal power and create credibility within yourself to set clear goals you WILL crush. This book is your platform to better understand your internal process. It is time to get ready to crush some goals!

<u>Some recurring themes to keep in mind:</u>
1. Stay in the action and out of the result
2. You must know your goal to understand your path
3. Don't wait for the perfect time
4. Willingness to embrace change creates opportunity
5. Structured flexibility
6. Consistency over perfection, always

SET THE STAGE

"The starting point is always now.
The end is up to you."

-Ron Kaufman

SET THE STAGE

Let's set the stage and lay the groundwork for effective goal setting. The following must be included to set and reach your goals:

1. Categories (activity/exercise, body composition/eating habits, etc.)
2. Benefits from consistently taking positive action
3. Rewards system (**"non-edible"**)
4. Challenges and Solutions (1:1 ratio)
5. Date of evaluation

Above are the sections you will use to fit the genre of your goals or the area of your life in which you want to make forward progress. The main component that will shape the tone of your process will be the chosen category or genre. For example, if I want to improve my self-esteem (genre), I might select categories around: building confidence, improving self-talk, and understanding gratitude. The selection of these categories will dictate the rest: benefits I will experience, the way I will reward myself, what potential challenges I might face, and how I will overcome those challenges. No matter the focus, there must be an evaluation date.

It's important to slow down and look inward so you can set **custom**, **realistic** (yet challenging), and **attainable** goals. We are often conditioned to do, what I like to call, "drive-by goal setting". This means that you have an idea of what you want to accomplish; and there is usually a good amount of intention. The missing piece is a clear plan of attack and a commitment to act in alignment with, and in support of that plan. The only way to create a clear plan of attack is to accept that change is required. You must do something different to get a different result. Your goals and action steps must be tailored so you create an opportunity to move forward with less hesitation. You must know your goal to understand your path.

Like any other skill, learning to slow down and adapt to change takes practice and consistency, effort, and self-discipline. Allow yourself patience and expect to make a few mistakes—it is the best way to learn, after all! Mistakes show you where your immediate course correction is needed, and that information is priceless.

> *If you are working with a coach, be sure you believe in and trust your chosen leader. Your coach should exude confidence and tact to help get you further than you would alone. You and your coach should be stronger together and be able to work as a unit. An accountability buddy can also help keep you on track. Neither is a must have, but coaches and accountability buddies are a great added layer to your support system.*

Honestly speaking, this process is tough. It requires emotional investment and demands consistent effort. I must add that even though it takes some hard work and focus, this process **does not** need to be overly complicated. This process only needs to be consistent more than it is inconsistent. These days, we are used to going so freaking fast that it's hard to slow down and be patient. You may not know what comes next or how to approach the process and that is where this tool will help to guide you. Starting is key! So how do we get the information to make the process clearer and more time-efficient? Enter, Coach Blaire.

> **Humor me for a moment and let's paint a little picture...**
>
> **If I challenged you to execute your ten-year plan in six months, would you think I was ridiculous? It's okay if your answer is, "Yes". Now, let's look at this scenario realistically. Realistically, it won't happen. Realistically, you will not *complete* your ten-year plan in six months. However, you will get a hell of a lot further than you would have without that lofty goal. Such a lofty goal would require you to execute laser focus, relentless intention, and follow through with zero hesitation or procrastination.**
>
> **This not to say that every goal you set should fall into the category of "ridiculous", but it is to say that you should push it! It's beneficial to set big goals that are difficult and require intentional effort. There is no perfect time so you might as well go for it!**

Before you start this process take a moment to turn inward for, my personal favorite, a "NO B.S. ASSESSMENT". A "NO B.S. ASSESSMENT" is an opportunity for transparency within yourself. You must be honest with yourself before you can bring about a "change mentality". Take a moment to reflect and get a better understanding of where you are now, what you are willing to do to reach your goals, and how committed to change you are willing to be.

Ask yourself the following questions and answer, honestly.	YES	NO
1. Are my goals a priority?	☐	☐
2. Am I willing to dig in and work as consistently as needed to reach my goals?	☐	☐
3. Am I willing to make mistakes and course correct along the way?	☐	☐
4. Am I willing to be coachable and try new approaches?	☐	☐
5. Do I see benefit in learning from someone else?	☐	☐
6. Am I willing to open up and be vulnerable with myself (and my coach, if applicable)?	☐	☐

If you answered "YES" to all the questions, then you are ready to move ahead!

If you answered "NO", I recommend you review and get familiar with this process. Understanding the process can help you identify areas you want to improve and behaviors you want to enhance. The awareness and personal transparency gained from the above questions provide you critical information to better understand yourself and your individual needs. You don't have to know everything to get started.

Continue your "NO. B.S. ASSESSMENT" by understanding your expectations.

Ask yourself and answer the following questions and, again, answer **honestly:**

1. What do you expect your experience will be when working toward your goal(s)?

2. How will you process your actual experience if it does not match your expected experience?

3. What do you expect of yourself/what standard will you hold yourself to?

Your answers to these questions help you understand your willingness and readiness to embrace change. There are no wrong answers, only valuable information so you have a better idea of where you are right now and what will shape your responses in the process ahead.

Your objective:

(1) Believe in yourself and your ability to prioritize what you want, and

(2) understand that it is possible to overcome your challenges and reach the goals you have effectively set!

CATEGORY 1: ACTIVITY AND EXERCISE

"If you aim for nothing, you'll hit it every time."

-Unknown

ACTIVITY AND EXERCISE

This first category segment focuses on increasing your activity and exercise levels on a consistent basis. Identify practical action steps that realistically fit your life. Think about pinpointing actions that you can consistently maintain. Note: It's okay if everything does not go exactly as planned. Because well... life! However, this roadmap **will** hold you more accountable than if you were not willing to create this structure. This is your opportunity to paint a clear picture, so that you build a platform to practice elevated self-monitoring and *structured flexibility*.

Self-monitoring is important whether you chose to work with a coach or not. Let's think about this pragmatically—even if you have a coach, you are not in contact with them 24/7. This means at some point you must step up and be accountable to yourself. You will build your accountability and self-credibility by selecting behaviors you can implement and will commit to following through, all the way. A coach will never be able to do it for you, but he/she/they can massively support your efforts and help you realize your strongest self. A solid coach should bring you an additional level of clarity, and support you through adversities and challenges along the way so you are best setup to meet your short-term goals.

> **Example of what NOT to do:**
>
> **Meet Kellen. Kellen has a full-time job, a family, and is in good health. He is currently working out zero days per week and thinks jumping into working out six days per week is the way to go—it's not. It sounds nice, but it is a huge shift in a short amount of time, and he will unlikely be able to sustain this. Kellen will be better served to think about simpler steps he can take to keep himself set up for success. Instead, he could set aside time three days per week at 45 minutes per session to exercise and one day per week to meal prep his lunch and all snacks for work for his 5-day work week. This allows him to gradually implement exercising regularly and get familiar with meal prepping; without needing to spend six hours in the kitchen cooking. This way he also limits his likelihood of overconsuming convenience foods at work (packaged snack bars, cookies, etc.). The idea is behavioral consistency in the long term.**

When introducing new behavioral enhancements into your daily routine, don't expect it to always be easy. During difficult times, focus on your actions so you don't become uninterested or too overwhelmed. Basically, you can put on **temporary** blinders to help you stay consistent with your actions. It is important to be honest with yourself about struggles and important to realize that most of the things you have achieved and/or developed in your life have not come easy. Introducing new behaviors is a change and it will take your consistent effort to build your new behavioral enhancements. Believe in your abilities, remember your priorities, and remind yourself this is worth it. You *can* do it.

Choose three specific ways you commit to increasing your activity, exercise, and fitness levels. If you prefer to fill out all five lines, I encourage you to go for it! If you feel that three new additions are too much to take on, simply choose one. Remember, even one behavioral enhancement can create a massive positive ripple effect. Simplicity is key.

See the following example.

ACTIVITY AND EXERCISE	
To increase my activity, exercise, and fitness levels I will take the following five steps:	
1. Walk for 30 min, 3x/week, Mon @ 5 pm, Wed @ 5 am, Fri @ 6 pm.	DD/MM/YYYY*
2. Classes at the gym, Tue & Thu, @ 8 am	DD/MM/YYYY
3. Strength program from Coach Blaire 3x/week, Mon, Wed, Sat, all @ 9 AM	DD/MM/YYYY
4. 20 min ankle mobility, 2x/wk, Tue & Sun	DD/MM/YYYY
5.	DD/MM/YYYY

The dates listed in this section should mirror when this commitment is being made.

NOW IT'S YOUR TURN

Ideas for inspiration:

- ✓ Consistency—Think about how many days per week you want to incorporate the action.

- ✓ Small add-ins—Think about what activities don't require a lot of setup or equipment that you may be able to add in for a short time (walking, squats, push-ups, etc.).
- ✓ Weight progression—Think about progressing the weights you may be lifting so you are able to get stronger in a more efficient period (within each set or over the course of a few weeks).
- ✓ Additional mobility & movement work—Think about additional stretching sessions or a movement flow that support your fitness or strength goals to keep you moving better for longer (customized from your coach or a yoga class, etc.).

Remember, every line item needs to be (1) specific, (2) measurable, and (3) customized for you.

EXAMPLE EXPLANATION

A line-item reading "walk more" would not fit the criteria. The intention is there, but it is short-lived. Ultimately, you will need to transform "walk more" into being *specific* and *measurable* so you can later evaluate to see how well this action is working for you and you can then course correct, if needed.

> **Be sure to:**
>
> **Ask yourself HOW and WHEN you will execute each line item as a sustainable part of your daily or weekly routine.**

Make it fit the criteria:

A *specific* and *measurable* line item might read "walk, 30 min, M W F". This combination of information sets the stage for a clear, accurate, and time-efficient evaluation. It also provides you a clear understanding of where to place this action in your schedule. If you want to kick it up a notch, add in what time of day you will plan to start each of those walks.

Example: walk, 30 min, M @ 5 pm, W @ 5 am, F @ 6 pm.

LIST YOUR LINE ITEMS BELOW

ACTIVITY AND EXERCISE
To increase my activity, exercise, and fitness levels I will take the following five steps:

1.	Date:
2.	Date:
3.	Date:
4.	Date:
5.	Date:

What to check for:

1. Specific subject matter/behavior or habit focus
2. Day, frequency, or duration during the week
3. Schedule (weekly/monthly)

GOAL WORKSHEET DRILL DOWN

1. Categories (activity/exercise, body composition/eating habits, etc.)
2. Benefits from consistently taking positive action
3. Rewards system (**"non-edible"**)
4. Challenges and Solutions (1:1 ratio)
5. Date of evaluation

THINGS TO REMEMBER:

1. Continue to stay a student of the process.
2. Remember **why** you want to reach these goals.
3. Be prepared to think outside the box.
4. Modify categories to fit your needs.
5. You are responsible for creating your roadmap, think about your needs and what is reasonable for **you**!

BENEFITS

"Stay focused on your goals, picture the end result and all the satisfaction it will bring."

-Unknown

BENEFITS

Benefits are the core connection points to your *why* and your *why* is the reason behind all this; it is more important than the goal itself. These positive benefits are what you will experience when you put in consistent work to maintain your "Activity and Exercise" goals/action steps listed in the previous section. If it is helpful for you, think of this as a place for attestation—your proof.

Sound cheesy to you? Keep going, anyway.

Practice compassion with yourself. Sometimes it is hard to allow yourself to feel what you need, when you need to, and then act accordingly, but this is your mission. When you start thinking about the benefits you will experience you might get a dose of reality and realize that this process requires effort! Thinking about the impacts of your efforts creates a sense of truth that helps you understand and more closely relate to your *why*—why any of this is meaningful to you.

Without this connectedness, you won't fully understand *why* it is worth putting forth focused effort to concentrate on your chosen action steps. Your emotional connection is how you prioritize your consistent efforts. It can be uncomfortable or feel unfamiliar, so be sure not to rush and allow yourself mental and emotional space to get your bearings and think clearly. This is how you practice compassion towards yourself. Take it slow and steady, no need for speed. Identify two benefits you will experience. If you can envision more than two benefits, feel free to add them.

Your objective:

Reach a better understanding of yourself and why your goals are worth working for!

Identify specific areas or situations where you will know you are living the benefits of your hard work.

See the following example.

The specific benefits that I will gain by taking these steps include:

1. I will be physically stronger when getting up off the floor after play time with my kids.

2. I will be more confident & less self-conscious during my weekly team meeting presentations at work.

3.

4.

Dates are not needed here (unless you want them to be) as these benefits correspond with the previous action items from the "Activity & Exercise" section.

NOW IT'S YOUR TURN

Ideas for Inspiration:

- ✓ Increases in fitness level—More endurance during the day.
- ✓ Ease of daily activities—Less pain and stiffness throughout the day.
- ✓ More self-confidence—Feeling proud of your ability and willingness to follow through.
- ✓ Energy sustainment—Less feelings of lethargy, no more "afternoon crash".
- ✓ Less anxiety due to creation of daily routine—a roadmap to help keep you focused during busy times.

Remember, every line item needs to be (1) specific, (2) measurable, and (3) customized for you.

EXAMPLE EXPLANATION

A line-item reading "I'll feel better" would not fit the beneficial criteria. You want to make sure that with this intention, you are supporting the identification and the *specificity* of your affirmations with a specific reason, experience, or period of time, etc.

> **Be sure to:**
>
> **Ask yourself HOW you will know you are experiencing the benefits in your daily life.**

Make it fit the criteria:

A *specific* and *measurable* line item might read, "I will be physically stronger when getting up off the floor after play time with my kids". This specific identification allows you to emotionally connect to the REASON behind the hard work. This is how you will experience, understand, and identify your individualized benefit. If you cannot visualize your positive experience, your hard work is unlikely to last. Visualize your real-life scenario so that you can foresee yourself living the benefit.

LIST YOUR LINE ITEMS BELOW

The specific benefits that I will gain by taking these steps include:

1.

2.

3.

4.

What to check for:

  1. Individualized—Check to be sure you make space for line-items into your current routine

  2. Specific item/action—List days of the week and/or time of day, plus activity duration

  3. How you will know—Check for the ways will you experience the benefit of actions you will take

THINGS TO REMEMBER:
1. Continue to stay a student of the process.
2. Remember **why** you want to reach these goals.
3. Be prepared to think outside the box.
4. Modify categories to fit your needs.
5. You are responsible for creating your roadmap, think about your needs and what is reasonable for **you**!

REWARDS

"Acknowledge all your small victories. They will eventually add up to something great."

-Kara Goucher

REWARDS

During this ongoing process, your proactive actions need to be self-acknowledged. Understand that rewards are ***not*** being used as something you have earned. You are working toward a mindset shift and it is another skill to strengthen. When you get to a place where you view rewards as acknowledgements of your positive efforts, you will more consistently experience improved mental, emotional and physical behaviors as well as stronger habits. It is no secret that many of us are not conditioned to practice rewarding ourselves this way. Rewards are ***not*** meant to be earned by perfection...

Does **consistent** perfection even exist?

When does your plan ever go perfectly?

If we were to base success on perfection, no one would ever be considered successful.

> **Example:** You choose to schedule a full body 90-minute massage as your reward because it is something you often don't prioritize, but you do enjoy it, and you know it will help move you closer to your fitness and other physical goals. Realistically, there is nothing holding you back from getting this massage *now* if you really want it. However, you are choosing to use this experience as a means to acknowledge your proactive actions. Moreover, making a mistake does not make your massage or intended reward null and void. If you are proactive more than you are not proactive, it is particularly important you acknowledge that effort and follow through with your intended reward. The follow through is key!

You don't need to be perfect to make progress. You aim high so that you push harder to get further than you would without the challenging goals—same as when you increase your weights to get stronger (also, recall the ten-year goal in six months example). You are responsible for pushing yourself and you need to be aware of when you do! When you give everything you can, and things still do not go as planned—what you have done is enough and it is as important to acknowledge as it is to keep going. This is also a mentality we are not often programmed to apply to our goals. Always practice consistency over perfection. Acknowledgement of your consistent efforts is a non-negotiable in this process.

The rewards you select don't have to be material items, although they can be if that is what floats your boat. Sometimes when you get a new game uniform, you just play better! Most importantly, the rewards you select need to be valued by you. There are a few stipulations. Your rewards need to be: (1) individualized, (2) important to you and, <u>most importantly, (3) all rewards must be **"non-edible"**!</u> You only need to select one item here and provide as much explanation or detail as possible. It can be helpful to make a list off to the side of other items you can pull from later, as you repeat this process.

<u>Another redundant, yet friendly, reminder: All rewards must be **"NON-EDIBLE"**!</u>

There's that "non-edible" thing again, so let's clarify...

Food is the ultimate knee-jerk reaction most people use to reward themselves. Before now, you may have associated unhealthy food with being a reward. How many times have you heard someone say they earned the ice cream they are about to eat because they worked hard all week (or even just did one hard work out)? It is critical to break that cycle. Instead of a reaction without much thought, you want to create strong intentional responses which support your goals.

> *Take a step outside and look inward, if you want to improve your health and body composition, how would unhealthy food make sense as a reward? That is not to say you should never consume unhealthy food...time, place, and intention make all the difference. A reward should enhance your progress, not slow it down or create more obstacles, where there were none. What most people have been conditioned to believe is that they have earned certain types of food. Not true.*

Newsflash: No one's actions earn them the right to eat any food!

When it comes to **any** type of food (healthy or unhealthy, nutrient dense or not), you either own the fact that you are going to consume any particular foods because you want to, or because you don't (which we forget is 100% okay and a healthy approach in moderation). If you meal prep regularly, you are choosing to eat those foods. If you don't meal prep, you are making that choice as well. And they are both okay! The focus needs to be on supporting your goals with synchronized actions. The last thing you want is to breed guilt after eating food with low nutritional value; or reinforce the idea that a donut or any other food with low nutritional value must be earned or, even worse, not allowed until a certain time! Truthfully, the donut tastes good, sometimes you just want one, and that is okay. The key is to not overdo it or eat to a point where your physical and/or emotional health is at risk. Emotional eating cycles make reaching goals and improving behaviors more difficult. This line of thinking can create a surplus of obstacles along the way.

Emotional eating is a separate conversation for another day. However, it is important to work with your mind set to begin moving away from (a) being emotionally connected to food and (b) the mentality that you "can't" have certain foods until it is earned. Get comfortable with the fact that you **do** deserve to acknowledge your efforts and it's **not** selfish to focus on yourself with this intention.

Your objective:

Identify situations, outings, or items that you appreciate and value and/or don't normally "do" for yourself.

Formulate your reward system below.

See the following example.

I will reward myself for successfully taking these steps by:
1. Designating 1 "kid free" hour to read my favorite book "add title here."
2. Purchasing 1 new pair of Nike shorts.
3.
4.

Dates are not needed here (unless you want them to be) as these benefits correspond with the previous action items from the "Activity & Exercise" section.

GOAL SETTING STRENGTH

NOW IT'S YOUR TURN

Ideas for Inspiration:

- ✓ Give undivided attention—schedule technology-free time with your kids or other family members (a reward for everyone!).
- ✓ Meditation—getting time alone with yourself is a great way to make your internal well-being a priority.
- ✓ Buy new workout shorts—look good, play well!
- ✓ Get a massage—great for recovery, relaxation, and injury prevention.
- ✓ Read a personal development book—There is never a bad time to grow.
- ✓ Go for a hike at a new location (day trip)—connecting with nature is good for all bodies (mental, emotional, spiritual, physical).

EXAMPLE EXPLANATION

"New clothes" is an unacceptable reward. The item works, but there is no *specificity* included. New clothes, gear or equipment can be a great way to acknowledge your efforts but make it specific. Another unacceptable reward is "no reward needed". It is hugely important to acknowledge your hard work, small wins, giant victories, consistency, and personal growth—you never need to be perfect. Rewards do not need to cost a lot of money either, which comes in handy during a pandemic when so many businesses and services are not available or safe.

> **Be sure to:**
>
> Ask yourself **HOW** you will reward yourself, what you value, what you enjoy and/or what you don't normally do for yourself.

Make it fit the criteria:

Instead of "new clothes", chose a *specific* item and brand that you have been wanting to add to your collection. A suitable line item might read "purchasing one new pair of Nike shorts!". If you know the specific style, add it in. Ladies, maybe you have been eyeing a particular brand of sports bra that, according to the reviews, will finally get "the girls" to stay in their lane. Guys, maybe you have been wanting to invest in a new manscaping product. Whatever it is, make it be just for you!

LIST YOUR LINE ITEMS BELOW

I will reward myself for successfully taking these steps by:
1.
2.
3.
4.

What to check for:

    1. Non-edible—food is not earned

    2. Individualized—make sure your reward is something you value

    3. Specific item or activity duration—size, brand, time, location, etc.

    4. Value (not monetary)—Why/how do you value the reward

THINGS TO REMEMBER:

    1. Stay a student of the process.

    2. Remember **why** you want to reach these goals.

    3. Be prepared to think outside the box.

    4. Modify categories to fit your needs.

    5. You are responsible for creating your roadmap, think about your needs and what is reasonable for **you**!

CATEGORY 2:
HEALTH AND EATING HABITS

"Set your goals high and don't stop until you get there."

-Bo Jackson

HEALTH AND EATING HABITS

***S**imple* action steps are *meaningful* and *highly effective*. Approach these line-items with confidence. Even though this specific goal-setting conversation is focused mainly on a strength and/or fitness program, it is no secret that nutrition is a big part of the process too.

> **You can also design this entire process around nutrition, from top to bottom, if you like.**

The same amount of *specificity* and *measurability* as in the very first section, "Activity and Exercise" is expected, here. Aim for two or three line-items that are (1) integrate-able (we can just pretend that's a word) into your current lifestyle and (2) simple to track.

See the following example.

HEALTH & EATING HABITS	
To eat healthier and achieve improved wellness, I will take the following five steps:	
1. Limit sugary dessert to 1x/week-Sat	DD/MM/YYYY*
2. Drink 1 additional glass of water before each meal, 7 days/week	DD/MM/YYYY
3. All snacks are raw vegetable based (2-3 per day), Mon-Fri	DD/MM/YYYY
4.	DD/MM/YYYY
5.	DD/MM/YYYY

*The dates listed in this section should mirror when this commitment is being made.

NOW IT'S YOUR TURN

Ideas for inspiration:

- ✓ Healthier snacks—raw fruits and veggies are healthy, easy to consume, and reduce meal prep time
- ✓ Increased water consumption—helps curb appetite, improves complexion and digestion, needed for optimum overall health

- ✓ Limiting sugar—reduces cravings and weight gain, prevents energy crash during the day
- ✓ Pre/post-workout snacks—supports recovery and muscle growth

<u>Remember, every line item needs to be (1) specific, (2) measurable, and (3) customized for you.</u>

EXAMPLE EXPLANATION

A line-item reading "eat more vegetables" would not suffice. We all know we should eat them, but vegetables are sometimes difficult to consume if you are not already used to doing so. You need *specificity* and *measurability*. Nutrition can be a major change for some individuals, so it's okay to start with something small.

> **Be sure to:**
> Ask yourself **HOW** you will execute each line item in your daily routine.

Make it fit the criteria:

You might consider replacing all snacks, or even just one snack per day, with a raw vegetable item five days per week. These small changes can reduce the need for additional meal prep or cook time and can also help replace food items such as chips and crackers because most raw vegetables have a sort of "crunch" which can mimic that of the unhealthy snacks (convenience foods) we normally grab on the run. This brings us back to *simple action steps are highly effective*.

You may also think about identifying a focused line-item for fruit (let's say apples) and set a goal to consume one apple per day for five days of the week. These are small attainable goals that are common knowledge when it comes to eating healthier, but sometimes not so obvious when we are in the thick of our own experience. You can also include water intake in this category. Note: A gallon of water is not the correct amount for everyone, so ask your coach if needed. If you know you are severely dehydrated on a regular basis (this may be a place for a "NO B.S. ASSMESSMENT"), add more water, consistently, each week, little by little. Keep your line items clear and *specific*.

LIST YOUR LINE ITEMS BELOW

HEALTH & EATING HABITS
To eat healthier and achieve improved wellness, I will take the following five steps:

1.	Date:
2.	Date:
3.	Date:
4.	Date:
5.	Date:

What to check for:

1. Specific subject matter—type of food, water consumption, post-workout nutrition, etc.

2. Day, frequency, or duration—meal prep times, duration

3. Schedule—which days of the week

Note: If you are living with a health condition that affects or restricts what/how you need to consume food and nutrients please be sure to speak with your doctor for further information and/or recommendations.

THINGS TO REMEMBER:

1. Stay a student of the process.

2. Remember **why** you want to reach these goals.

3. Be prepared to think outside the box.

4. Modify categories to fit your needs.

5. You are responsible for creating your roadmap, think about your needs and what is reasonable for **you**!

ADDITIONAL GOALS

"If they think your dreams are crazy, show them
what crazy dreams can do."

-Sue Bird

ADDITIONAL GOALS
SLEEP, SMOKING, ALCOHOL INTAKE, POSITIVE SELF-TALK

This is your opportunity to take the blinders off and look at other areas of your life that you want to strengthen during this process. These other areas should still support your health and fitness and/or strength goals. "Additional Goals" may seem superfluous, but what you write here can create a ripple effect that will strengthen the entire foundation of your outlook, perceptions, and attitude. No matter how you approach this section, be sure to focus on targets **not** directly related to movement or food.

Some areas that may be helpful are (a) setting a consistent sleep time, (b) limiting screen time to create space in the day for movement, (c) improving positive self-talk, or (d) limiting alcohol intake. I suggest at least two line-items be identified, *specific* and *measurable*, of course. As this section can also be uncomfortable and often feel vulnerable when topics such as self-confidence or self-talk comes up, be sure you are cognizant of continuing to lean into any discomfort, and staying present, as you work through insecurities or internal struggles. The experienced discomfort/"emotional nakedness" is temporary.

You can roll your eyes again at the idea of positive self-talk. You may think it sounds silly or that you will feel weird repeating a statement of encouragement to yourself in the mirror or into your cell phone camera every day. But guess what? IT FREAKING WORKS! It doesn't have to be a monologue, for crying out loud, just a few words or a sentence that helps establish a subconscious belief that you want to uphold. You might feel "emotionally naked" at first, but when you give yourself a chance to build this skill consistently, and over time, it does get easier. And guess what? Negative self-talk is more unconscious and automatic versus positive self-talk, which is more conscious and proactive. So, give it a shot, I challenge you.

See the following example.

ADDITIONAL GOALS	
(Sleep, Smoking, Alcohol Intake, Positive Self-talk, etc.)	
1. Recite my mantra aloud 7 days/wk: "The way I speak to myself matters"	DD/MM/YYYY*
2. Consistent wake-sleep schedule: wake @ 6 am, sleep at 10 pm, 7 days/wk	DD/MM/YYYY
3.	DD/MM/YYYY

*The dates listed in this section should mirror when this commitment is being made.

NOW IT'S YOUR TURN

Ideas for Inspiration:

- ✓ Bedtime routine—helps improve circadian rhythm for restful sleep and better recovery.
- ✓ Positive self-talk/daily mantras—actively shift to improve your subconscious view of yourself and what you are capable of handling.
- ✓ Morning meditation—helps set intention and focus for a productive day.
- ✓ Reduced smoking and/or alcohol consumption—healthy for quite obvious reasons.

Remember, every line item needs to be (1) specific, (2) measurable and, (3) customized for you.

EXAMPLE EXPLANATION

A line-item reading "positive self-talk" would not suffice. Always verify your three main touch points, *specificity, measurability,* and *customization* are included.

> **Be sure to:**
> **Ask yourself HOW you will manifest each itemized goal in your daily routine.**

Make it fit the criteria:

With more specificity the line might read "Recite my mantra aloud 1x/day, 7 days/week: The way I speak to myself matters". This, again, allows you to have a clear and concise goal that is manageable and can have a huge constructive effect on your outcomes.

LIST YOUR LINE ITEMS BELOW

ADDITIONAL GOALS
(Sleep, Smoking, Alcohol Intake, Positive Self-talk, etc.)

1.   Date:

2.   Date:

3.   Date:

What to check for:

    1. Individualized—does this action pertain to me

    2. Enhances daily schedule—will this action help me be more efficient in this process

    3. Increases self-awareness/confidence—will this action help me improve my confidence and self-credibility

---

THINGS TO REMEMBER:

    1. Stay a student of the process.

    2. Remember **why** you want to reach these goals.

    3. Be prepared to think outside the box.

    4. Modify categories to fit your needs.

    5. You are responsible for creating your roadmap, think about your needs and what is reasonable for **you**!

CHALLENGES AND SOLUTIONS

"There are always going to be obstacles that come in your way. Stay positive."

-Michael Phelps

CHALLENGES AND SOLUTIONS

CHALLENGES

We all have them. The focus then becomes, not letting those challenges prevent you from reaching your goals. But how? Sometimes challenges come from outside circumstances or uncontrollable circumstances; and sometimes your challenges come from within yourself. When you face and manage your internal challenges, you create the opportunity to manage your external challenges more effectively because you are *idling lower*—with less stress and worry. *Idling lower* is simply a by-product of managing our stress and anxiety levels effectively and consistently. This management can be in the form of exercise, meditation, breathing exercises, reading, listening to music, etc. Your management methods are individualized and are found by trial and error and then cemented by repeated practice. You must first face your internal challenges before you can manage them and move forward.

> *Remember you are not alone. We all have obstacles, demons, baggage, trauma, and fears to face and work through. You will be stronger, in the end, for being willing to acknowledge them, stand toe-to-toe with them, and transcend them. You have the ability to not let your internal challenges dictate your results, never forget that.*

Some external factors are completely out of your control (i.e.: how the government decides to handle the COVID-19 pandemic that started in 2020). Other external challenges may easily come to mind because they are, very often, the reasoning you associate with "can't"—can't workout or get to the places you say you want to be because of your work schedules or family duties, etc. There is definite legitimacy with any challenge you identify so be sure not to minimize how you feel and continue practicing compassion with yourself. Do remember, you are the priority, and this is a time to make your life about you! It is not selfish for you to take the time to set goals for yourself and work with relentless intention to achieve those goals. You are worth the investment.

Additionally, identifying challenges can sometimes feel like a dumping ground, or a place where you "vent". Let it happen. You can sort through it later if lots of information is flowing or if your thoughts are coming out in an ambiguous way. I can't stress this enough, if the information is coming out, let it! If you are struggling to identify any challenges, stop for a moment and assess if you are holding back out of fear or insecurity.

SELF-SABOTAGE.

You have probably practiced self-sabotage, at some point in your life, but whether you acknowledge it is a different story. This concept of "self-sabotage" does not come with super great sentiments so you may tend to avoid it completely. Nobody loves addressing the fact that they may be the one thing stopping their own personal growth and success.

Success can be scary, there's no way around that.

Success can make you more vulnerable to others and more vulnerable to yourself.

Success can come with added responsibility, pressure, or judgment, etc.

Success can be overwhelming, no doubt.

My goal is to shift perception paradigms, so you understand *why* you are hesitant to act. This information and self-awareness help you course correct more than anything else.

The strongest among us are willing to quiet their ego and allow humility and vulnerability into their process. We must step up and be willing to take responsibility for ourselves. These are characteristics not of weakness, but of immense strength.

Don't be surprised if you have thoughts of "self-sabotage" or "lack of support from partner or spouse" because you are headed toward a breakthrough! Breakthroughs are epic and can feel like an "aha moment" (insert lightbulb emoji here). The most important part of this moment is what you decide to do with your realization. Sometimes our light bulb moments preface a tough situation, and you may be faced with a challenging decision about how you will choose to respond. You may feel uneasy and uncomfortable, but lean into those feelings, you will then have the power to transcend and work through them.

Create an outline of what you foresee could produce challenges while you are working to reach your goals (right now, goals = all goals/line items listed during the previous parts of this process). The information provided in this section will vary from person to person. If you are discussing with your accountability buddy or completing this with a friend, be sure not to compare yourself and keep focus on your own experience. It is important to allow yourself the opportunity to answer honestly and completely. Afterall, there isn't a "wrong" obstacle. Assess two concrete areas for challenges, depending on what your personal journey includes. These can be: (1) external (i.e.: work schedule), and (2) internal (i.e.: lack of self-confidence). These two areas may produce more than two challenges so, if you feel you can include more than two, double check to make sure they are *specific* and truly an obstacle for you. Provide as much *specificity* as possible with each line item.

Note: You will not be able to foresee every single challenge that you will face but identifying the ones you *can* foresee will greatly increase your chance of success and adherence to your plan.

See the following example.

CHALLENGES:
The challenges I will face in reaching my goals include:

1. My rotating work schedule is never the same 2 weeks in a row. Very difficult to have a set time to exercise.

2. Keep up with the extracurricular and academic schedule of my 3 kids (baseball, tutoring, dance, piano).

3. I don't feel I deserve to be successful in reaching these goals.

4.

NOW IT'S YOUR TURN

Ideas for Inspiration:

- ✓ Turn inward and evaluate self-discipline/willingness to prepare—can you improve your daily routine? Are you willing to try new methods of preparation?

- ✓ Assess work schedule or extracurricular activities of your children—plan ahead whenever possible, so you can block out time for the immoveable obligations and then be able to physically see where you can take back more control.
- ✓ Observe your fears or concerns—it's ok to be scared! Acknowledge them so you are aware and therefore have the power to choose how much energy you invest.

<u>Remember, every line item needs to be (1) specific (2) measurable...challenges should be innately customized.</u>

EXAMPLE EXPLANATION

As previously discussed, you will likely think of work schedules or obligations for your kiddos (or other family members) as some of the challenges that make reaching your goals more difficult. Note that "work schedule" is not *specific* or *measurable*. Another common response is a general feeling of resistance. AKA: "I have no obstacles". To which I, politely, call bull! If you find yourself in either of these scenarios, start with the low-lying fruit of work schedules, etc. and make an effort to go further below the surface each time you repeat the evaluation process. (The evaluation process is coming up!) This path of effective goal setting is yours to make, what and how you need in order to be set up for success. When you allow yourself to explore your internal experiences, you create a space to make solid and lasting changes.

Note: You can re-write this section at any time, even before the evaluation date. BUT you must be willing to be fully transparent with yourself.

> **If needed, be sure to:**
>
> **Ask yourself HOW an obstacle makes your goals difficult to reach, specifically.**

Make it fit the criteria:

Instead of "work schedule", the line item might read "My rotating work schedule is never the same 2 weeks in a row. Very difficult to have a set time to exercise". This provides you some insight into *how* this obstacle makes reaching your goals more challenging. Therefore, you have a clearer understanding of what you are trying to work through. Repeat the concept of applying your "how" for all obstacles you can foresee.

LIST YOUR LINE ITEMS BELOW

CHALLENGES:
The challenges I will face in reaching my goals include:

1.

2.

3.

4.

What to check for:

    1. Individualized—Is this a challenge specific to me and my life?

    2. Specific—What about the obstacle, in particular, makes it challenging?

    3. Meaningful or impactful to growth—If managed differently, could this have a more positive effect on my life?

SOLUTIONS

Solutions provide you a gateway to **make change**. The tricky part is that you have to create your own solutions. Many people tend to focus on the negative, like another knee jerk reflex, but this your opportunity to live and practice your *how*! Your "how" is created by the way you choose to respond and not simply react to your challenges. And, of course, you need a little self-discipline.

    Once you have identified challenges, try to understand *how* each of those challenges will be managed (a response) ...not *if* they will be managed (a reaction). This management is what most of us associate with overcoming, and this is hard. Period. But you can do hard things! From the start, I committed to pulling back the curtain and removing the frou-frou sugar coating and I intend to follow through. The solutions you commit to do not act as a guarantee, but more as a reminder—you already know you **can** transcend your obstacles.

When you think outside the box to find solutions, consider ways to *simplify* your obstacles. Your solutions don't need to be complicated, only customized. For example, if you don't currently work out or not very consistently, don't try to move mountains overnight by jumping into a six day per week exercise routine (remember the previous example of Kellen). It won't get you any closer to where you need to be, because it will be super difficult to adhere to over the long haul. This then leads to feelings of inadequacy and overwhelming impatience and then to quitting on that plan. Instead, work on creating solutions. Your solutions come from behavioral enhancements and challenge simplification. Our lofty achievable goals should be made of bite-sized pieces to digest incrementally along the way.

Real-life example:

Often, there is an association with time and exercise—as in, a workout must or should be 60-90 minutes. Not true. When you have this time association with exercising and don't see any possible way to make 60-90 minutes magically become available in your daily schedule at the desired frequency, you are literally trying to smush that idea into a schedule where it doesn't sensibly fit. Instead, think to simplify.

Let's say a realistic amount of time you want to work up to dedicating to exercising is 30 minutes per session. Maybe, you try a workout for 20-25 minutes, three days per week to start. Most of us can manage that when we operate with a little self-discipline. Over the next few weeks, you evaluate and come to the conclusion that it wasn't super easy but was still manageable and allowed you to do more consistent activity than you had done in years. So, it's working!

After a few more weeks, perhaps you add a few minutes and go for your goal of 30 minutes of exercise per session, keeping the frequency at three days per week. During the next few weeks, maybe you find it exceedingly difficult to get the 30 minutes in consistently versus the previous weeks at 25 minutes per workout. How can you make 30 minutes fit into your daily routine?

Instead of starting over completely with a different type of workout or stopping all together due to frustration, impatience, or annoyance, ask yourself *how* you can make this obstacle simpler? One option is to split it. If you could manage 25 minutes at once, you can for sure manage 15 minutes at once. Piece of cake, right? 15 minutes in the morning and 15 minutes in the evening, gives you your full 30 minutes. Boom.

Is this the number one choice for setup and execution? Probably not.

Is this the way you expected your workouts to look? Probably not.

Does this setup allow you to continue reaching for your goals in a way that is *specific* to your needs, *measurable* during your evaluation, and *customized* to fit your lifestyle? One million gazillion percent, YES!

Now, comes a choice. A choice to continue or not, when the actual experience is different from the imagined experience.

Don't ever assume "thinking outside the box" must equal grandiose, large, or complicated approaches. The purpose of "thinking outside the box" is finding ways to make your path more easily traveled by you. Ultimately, focus on how you can cut your obstacle into smaller pieces to help create your solutions! It may not always be your first choice, but sometimes you gotta do what you gotta do.

Remember, customized not complicated.

It is not unusual to feel a bit drained at this point if you have really been going for it because you have been pulling more from your emotional tank than you probably anticipated. It's okay! Take a breath and keep going! Keep in mind, in both thought-process and in action, *consistency over perfection*.

See the following example.

> **SOLUTIONS:**
>
> *I will overcome these challenges by:*
>
> 1. As soon as my work schedule is released, <u>*I will*</u> schedule my workout times for the next 2 weeks—3 sessions per week.
>
> 2. <u>*I will*</u> work in carpools 2 days per week (Tues & Thurs) to limit my drive time and adhere to what my own needs are.
>
> 3. <u>*I commit*</u> to reading my mantra aloud 1x/day & make a list to keep in my phone of all the reasons why I ACCEPT success in this area of my life.
>
> 4.

Dates are not needed here (unless you want them to be) as these challenges and solutions correspond with the previous action items from the "Activity & Exercise' section."

NOW IT'S YOUR TURN

Ideas for Inspiration:

- ✓ Time blocking or making a more specific schedule—Try different approaches to your daily preparation and organization.
- ✓ Setting phone or computer alarms as a reminder to get going—Great for busy and working humans!
- ✓ Deciding to believe in yourself!—No one can choose this for you.

<u>Remember, every line item needs to be (1) specific, (2) measurable, and (3) customized for you.</u>

EXAMPLE EXPLANATION

Each identified challenge should be accompanied by a method to overcome it. For example, "get organized" will not make the cut. Where is the *specific measurability*?

> **Be sure to:**
>
> **Ask yourself HOW you will face and maneuver your roadblocks, one-by-one.**

Make it fit the criteria:

A more *specifically measurable* solution might be "as soon as my work schedule is released, **I will** schedule my workout times for the next two weeks—three sessions per week." This gives you a specific task to complete to make the obstacle of your work schedule more manageable. Take a moment to be sure you are approaching your obstacles and solutions in a pragmatic way that you genuinely believe in. The more detail you can get down on paper, the better your result will be. When in doubt, ask yourself "how"?

LIST YOUR LINE ITEMS HERE

SOLUTIONS:
I will overcome these challenges by:
1.

2.

3.

4.

What to check for:

1. 1:1, "challenge" to "solution" ratio—Each challenge needs an intentional solution

2. Specificity—Each solution needs to be specific and measurable

3. Realistic intention to commit—Make sure solutions are reasonable and ultimately smooth out the process for you

4. Action step(s)—Identify as many specifics as possible **before** doing it so you have a safety net if you get or feel stuck

---

GOAL WORKSHEET DRILL DOWN

1. Categories (activity/exercise, body composition/eating habits, etc.)

2. Benefits from consistently taking positive action

3. Rewards system (**"non-edible"**)

4. Challenges and Solutions (1:1 ratio)

5. Date of evaluation

THINGS TO REMEMBER:

1. Stay a student of the process.

2. Remember **why** you want to reach these goals.

3. Be prepared to think outside the box.

4. Modify categories to fit your needs.

5. You are responsible for creating your roadmap, think about your needs and what is reasonable for **you**!

EVALUATION OF GOALS

"I'm reflective in the sense that I learn to move forward. I reflect with a purpose."

-Kobe Bryant

EVALUATION OF GOALS

The hard stuff you put off is holding you back from moving forward! Reflect and evaluate with a purpose, just as the late, great Kobe Bryant did. If you are going to put in the effort to outline this path, you owe it to yourself to check-in and see how it's going. Without periodic evaluations, you won't be able to clearly see what is working, what is not working, or what is "sort of" working so you can improve, and course correct along the way. This is the culmination of creating the baseline to provide yourself the opportunity for the best possible outcomes, down the road. This evaluation marks the end of the first, of many, cycles to get further than you would have gone without intentional goal setting. The ability and willingness to evaluate your actions and mindset is critical when deciphering if course correction or additional support is needed to continue enhancing your behaviors and habits. You must know your goal to understand your path.

Your evaluation should come roughly four weeks after the conclusion of this process. The four-week marker is pliable based on your goals and your lifestyle. This means, you can evaluate your progress sooner or later than four weeks if that better suits you—but be sure not to delay needlessly or indefinitely. Given that you are focusing on short-term actions to help support long-term goals, you want to stay within two to six weeks between evaluations. You want enough time to put your focus points into practice so you get an idea of what is working and, conversely, what could use a little makeover. You also want to make sure you don't go with SO much time between your evaluations that you create poor habits or routines that simply aren't supporting your forward progress.

Set your evaluation date and sign. Do not take this lightly. Even if you are doing this on your own, without a coach, this is how you are sealing the deal and committing to follow through with this path you have just created. Think it's dumb? Sign it anyway. If you are creating this path with a coach, you absolutely need to have him/her/them sign too.

See the following example.

Evaluation of goals:

I/We plan to review these goals on:_____ DD/MM/YYYY_____

_____

_____*Blaire Camarda*_____   ____DD/MM/YYYY_____
                Signature   Date

_____
              Trainer Signature   Date
               (if applicable)

NOW IT'S YOUR TURN

Be sure to fill in **all** applicable information. Do not start cutting corners, now!

EXAMPLE EXPLANATION

During your evaluation, assess if any improvements or changes need to be made and record them. This is also a time to reinforce your reward. If consistent and positive (**not perfect**) action steps were taken to get closer to meeting goals your reward is to be utilized. You should re-create this worksheet, from the beginning, about once every three months. As short-term goals should, ideally, be accomplished (or getting darn close), new habits should be forming, and an innate internal readiness to move ahead should be presenting itself.

    This timeframe ought to provide an opportunity for you to progress to new levels of self-confidence and self-credibility. You should see improvements physically, mentally, and emotionally, and want to continue pushing yourself closer to your potential. Ultimately, you need to fit every piece of this puzzle to match the needs and consistency of your life and schedule, so it is **manageable**. Be sure to set your next date as you finish each evaluation cycle. You will not magically remember to go back to it in four weeks. Write it down, now!

COMPLETE YOUR EVALUATION COMMITMENT BELOW

Evaluation of goals:

I/We plan to review these goals on:_____

_____

_____

              Signature   Date

_____

       Trainer Signature   Date
        (if applicable)

What to check for:
- ✓ A date roughly 3-5 weeks out for evaluation of goals
- ✓ Signatures from you and your trainer/accountability buddy (if applicable)
- ✓ Date the agreement was made
- ✓ Mark your calendar!

RECAP

"The man on top of the mountain
did not fall there."

-Vince Lombardi

RECAP

Overall

You don't have to have everything figured out right from the start. You DO need to know your goal to understand your path. Whether or not you feel 100% ready, just go for it! Don't wait for the perfect time, it doesn't exist. However, following the steps laid out here will help set you up for ultimate success. No matter what, you must be courageous enough to start! Create and execute your path with confidence, conviction, and a little self-discipline.

Building Credibility

Do hard things! Doing hard things is the best way to build the credibility and belief in yourself that you can achieve your goals. The way you do that is by following through with the commitments you have made to yourself—actually doing the things you say you are going to do. Understand your expections—(1) what you expect from yourself/the standard you will hold yourself to and (2) how you will process your actual experience if it is different than what you are expecting. This is how you learn to take responsibility for your actions and hold yourself accountable. This builds your self-credibility.

Emotional Nakedness

With practice you will get comfortable celebrating your efforts and accomplishments—feeling emotionally naked doesn't last forever. Lean into the discomfort and know it is temporary and safe to keep going.

Structured Flexibility

Operate from a position of *structured flexibility* so you can apply this system to ANY goal you have and streamline the process to make it a reality. Regardless of the focus of your ultimate goal, the steps you create must always be: (1) specific, (2) measurable, and (3) individualized to you. This process does not need to be complicated, only customized for your needs and your life. When in doubt, ask yourself WHAT steps you will take and HOW you will implement those steps into your daily or weekly routine?

Additional Goals

Your "additional goals" hold a lot of clout! Look inward to face your "stuff" and break through your self-inflicted barriers. This is a great place for mantras, affirmations, and positive self-talk.

Evaluation

When you evaluate your direction and make course corrections, set your next evaluation date. Don't assume you will just happen to remember...you won't! Keep your goals a priority and allow yourself to pursue them with tenacious intention. Mark your calendar!

SECTIONS AND AREAS OF FOCUS:

1. Categories (activity/exercise, body composition/eating habits, etc.)

2. Benefits from consistently taking positive action

3. Rewards system (**"non-edible"**)

4. Challenges and Solutions (1:1 ratio)

5. Date of evaluation

THINGS TO REMEMBER:

1. Stay a student of the process.

2. Remember **why** you want to reach these goals.

3. Be prepared to think outside the box.

4. Modify categories to fit your needs.

5. You are responsible for creating your roadmap, think about your needs and what is reasonable for **you**!

NEVER FORGET HOW WILDELY CAPABLE YOU ARE!

GOAL WORKSHEET

LONG-TERM HEALTH/FITNESS/STRENGTH GOAL (6-12 MONTHS):

_____
_____

ACTIVITY AND EXERCISE
To increase my activity, exercise, and fitness levels I will take the following five steps:

1.	Date:
2.	Date:
3.	Date:
4.	Date:
5.	Date:

The specific benefits that I will gain by taking these steps include:

1.
2.
3.
4.

I will reward myself for successfully taking these steps by:

1.
2.
3.
4.

HEALTH & EATING HABITS
To eat healthier and achieve improved wellness, I will take the following five steps:

1.	Date:
2.	Date:
3.	Date:
4.	Date:
5.	Date:

ADDITIONAL GOALS:
Sleep, Smoking, Alcohol Intake, Positive Self-talk, etc.

1.	Date:
2.	Date:
3.	Date:

CHALLENGES:
The challenges I will face in reaching my goals include:

1.

2.

3.

4.

SOLUTIONS:
I will overcome these challenges by:

1.

2.

3.

4.

Evaluation of goals:

I/We plan to review these goals on:_____

_____

_____

Signature   Date

_____

Trainer Signature   Date
(if applicable)

*T*hank for you taking the time to read this book and for making the investestment in yourself. I would love honest feedback about this, and all books in the series so they continue to be made the most comprehensive tools for you. Your views not only impact other reader's decisions on which tools they use, but also matter to me as well. Thank you, again. I appreciate you.

Leave your review at: *https://www.amazon.com/~/e/B088T2ZYFH*

ACKNOWLEDGEMENTS

Thank you to those that helped make this book come to life. Thanks to my family (Mom, Dad, Al, and Court) for the time spent providing feedback and incredible support during this process. To Anastasia for, again, making this thing **real**! I've learned much from you and can't wait for the next one. To Coach Glabb, for the chats, support, and belief in me and my ability to tackle this project. Thank you, Tammy, for your profound insight and ability to help me get unstuck.

I want to thank all my clients who have been willing to share their stories and experiences, to tap into their potential and allow me to support them along their health and fitness journey. Only when you committed, did you create action and understanding of your goals and where you want to be. Thank you for going for it! You are the true inspiration for this book.

I couldn't have done this without any of you. This is the next step of a long journey, and I couldn't have done it without any of you (insert heart emoji, here).

ALSO AVAILABLE ON AMAZON

PAPERBACK AND E-BOOK

"I would definitely recommend this to my ladies who struggle with their own self-sabotaging tactics!"

-T.L., C.S.C.S

"Coach Blaire's success comes from hard work, knowledge of her skills and a natural ability to teach. You are in good hands with Coach Blaire."

-Tammy M.

Made in the USA
Middletown, DE
02 April 2023

28083542R00042